NO PARTICULAR PLACE TO GO

Sermons For Sundays After Pentecost (Middle Third) Cycle B, First Lesson Texts

Timothy J. Smith

D1374048

CSS Publishing Company, Inc., Lima, Ohio

Copyright © 1996 by
CSS Publishing Company, Inc.
Lima, Ohio

Scripture quotations are from the *New Revised Standard Version of the Bible*, copyright 1989 by the Division of Christian Education of the National Council of the Churches of Christ in the USA. Used by permission.

Library of Congress Cataloging-in-Publication Data

Smith, Timothy J., 1957-
    No particular place to go : sermons for Sundays after Pentecost (middle third) : Cycle B, first lesson texts / Timothy J. Smith.
        p.   cm.
    ISBN 0-7880-0781-5 (pbk.)
    1. Story sermons. 2. Sermons, American. 3. Bible. O.T. — Sermons. 4. Church year sermons. I. Title.
BV4307.S7S65   1996
252'.6—dc20
                                                                            96-4986
                                                                            CIP

This book is available in the following formats, listed by ISBN:
    0-7880-0781-5   Book
    0-7880-0782-3   IBM 3 1/2
    0-7880-0783-1   Mac
    0-7880-0784-X   Sermon Prep

PRINTED IN U.S.A.

To my family,
Donna, Rebecca and Matthew —
a constant source of inspiration

To the congregations
which I have served as pastor

Table Of Contents

Introduction

Ridin' along in my automobile,
my baby beside me at the wheel,
I stole a kiss at the turn of a mile,
my curiosity runnin' wild,
cruisin' and playin' the radio,
with no particular place to go ...

Chuck Berry's 1964 hit song, "No Particular Place to Go," describes the life of many of us in the last years of the twentieth century. We are cruising down the highway of life at breakneck speed, stereo blasting, not quite sure where we are going. It is a universal experience to search for meaning in our lives. The question becomes how do we find meaning. Many persons have unsuccessfully tried to find meaning in their lives through various means, all of which have one thing in common: they did not deliver what they promised. Persons are left with that empty feeling. Some turn to deadly addictions to find meaning. Others turn to the latest fad, hoping somewhere to find the long sought-after meaning in their lives. The result is that people are walking around rather aimlessly these days, desperately looking for some place to go — but are having difficulty finding that place. People are so desperate to feel something in their lives that they are willing to try just about anything.

We are able to discover meaning in life within the pages of our Bibles. In this collection of Old Testament sermons, I attempt to connect the modern listener with the ancient characters who do have something to say to us today. In some circles the Old Testament is viewed as irrelevant, having nothing to offer the modern person who is faced with a multitude of problems our ancient ancestors could not even imagine. The characters of the

Old Testament can help us out of our misdirection if not by leading the way then by their failed example. Some situations never change.

During my early pastorates I experimented with narrative preaching, telling the biblical story in a fresh way. My goal was and continues to be having biblical characters leap off the pages of the old book to intersect with our lives. While not everyone in the churches I have pastored has been enthusiastic with my attempts at narrative preaching, I will say that the majority have gained new insights from the scripture they did not think possible.

Stories have power and stories touch people's lives in ways nothing else can. Complementing my narrative style of biblical preaching with real life stories enables people to interact with the scripture in a stimulating way. I am often amazed how my stories touch the lives of people. Someone will speak with me and say, "You remember that story you told ...." Most of the time I do not remember specific stories yet I realize that story has impacted the person's life in a positive, sometimes transforming, way. It is as if God spoke to that person through that story. People take stories home with them and think about them time and time again. This past year a girl in my confirmation class stated that she likes having stories in the sermons since "it allows you to draw your own conclusions." Stories intersect with person's lives; they can identify with the struggles and joys of others.

In an age where people are searching for meaning, we have a story to tell. A story that changes lives, a story of our God who loves us no matter where we have been or what trouble we have found ourselves in.

John C. Holbert, in his excellent book, *Preaching Old Testament,* writes: "For the Hebrew Bible, to tell the story is the most urgent activity of the faithful. Theologically speaking, the Hebrew Bible insists that all of God's people are charged to become tellers of the story of God."

We have a new generation that has never heard the "old, old story." It is both our privilege and our responsibility to share that story.

Timothy J. Smith
September 1995

No Particular Place To Go

It was the last week of summer when some boys who had spent the summer playing together became restless and bored. School would start the next week and they found themselves not knowing what to do, wearied from all the other summer activities that they had enjoyed. On a hot August afternoon the boys decided to play a round of pitch and putt at a local golf course. At least this would give them something different to do and keep them from complaining to their parents about how bored they were — which was what they had been doing for days.

At the end of their rather lackluster round of golf, the boys noticed some soft drinks stored in a shed. It was obvious that the soft drinks were intended for the vending machine and that someone must have been refilling the machine when he was called to another task. Certainly he didn't want to leave soft drinks out in the open. With no one watching, the boys stole several bottles, stashing them in their golf bags. They left the golf course without being caught.

In the cool of the evening the boys sat in the shade drinking their soda pop in a carefree manner. Doug's father saw him and asked where he had gotten it. It didn't take too long before the father realized that the boys had stolen the soft drinks from the golf course. The father lectured the boys and told Doug to go immediately to his room as punishment. He told them they should be ashamed of what they had done. The next day Doug's father came home for lunch to take him back to the golf course so that he could apologize to the owner for stealing soda pop, return the unopened bottles, and pay for the ones he had already drunk. Doug said he didn't know what was worse, being caught by his father or having to confront the man he had stolen from. It was a lesson Doug would remember the next time he was tempted to do something he knew was wrong.

Mighty King David had experienced a meteoric ride to power and fame: a lowly shepherd boy was anointed king. It seemed that everything David did was a great success; all his battles ended with a decisive victory. He united the two kingdoms, he returned the famed ark of the covenant to Jerusalem, and he even talked about building a new temple to house it. The people just loved him, giving him the highest approval rating of any king. To the people David could do no wrong. A problem arose, however, when King David began thinking that he could do no wrong.

David grew restless and bored at the palace. Our lesson opens in the spring of the year, "when kings go out to battle." But David did not go out to war, instead he remained in his palace, rather bored by the whole thing. In his younger days David would have been right in the middle of the action, alongside his generals. David had a reputation for leading by example. Now a mid-life crisis struck David and he no longer desired to go to battle. He lingered at the palace with days of endless boredom. Besides he was rather secure in his position; it wasn't as though someone would challenge him.

Late one afternoon, after rising from a nap, David took a stroll on the roof of the palace. As David gazed out over his kingdom he couldn't help but be impressed with what he saw. Standing on his rooftop, David took a deep breath and momentarily felt pretty good. As David looked out over his kingdom he couldn't help but notice a woman bathing on a nearby rooftop. During the hot months wealthy people would eat, sleep, and apparently bathe on the roof where it was cooler. David, who hadn't felt much of anything in his restless state, suddenly became possessed by the beauty of the unknown woman. Upon inquiry, he discovered that the woman was Bathsheba, the wife of one of his soldiers, Uriah the Hittite. David became consumed with one thought: he must have this woman. David acted in a thoughtless, completely spontaneous manner — he must have this woman no matter what — without even considering the consequences. Mighty King David, who in the eyes of the people could do no wrong, committed a sinful act, breaking one of the ten commandments.

David's sinful act would be the beginning of his downfall. Life would never again be the same for David and his entire family or for the whole kingdom. We are accountable to God for the way we live our lives. Evidently David forgot about God since he was of the opinion that he could do no wrong. What David did was wrong; it was abuse of his power as king.

Before too long Bathsheba sent word to David, "I am pregnant." What no one else could do, Bathsheba did with only three words. She caused King David to panic. What David did was bad enough, but he would only make matters worse by devising a plan to cover up his act. David was still in control of the situation, at least that was what he thought. David immediately sent for Uriah, Bathsheba's husband. If he could get Uriah to spend some time with his wife, there would be no suspicion when neighbors saw her with child. Uriah had been off fighting the king's battle for quite some time, he would certainly appreciate some rest and relaxation. At least that was what David was counting on.

Even though King David sinned, he thought he would get away with it; after all he was king. David would painfully discover that his sin would cause more trouble than he ever dreamed. It doesn't matter if we are kings or ordinary people, when we sin there are bound to be consequences to follow. There are always consequences to our actions.

Let me tell you about someone who made this discovery in her life. Her name is Pat. She had committed a crime, was convicted, and sentenced to serve time in jail. It was too much for her, so she ran away, trying desperately to escape from the consequences. It's always easier to run from the past than to confront it head on. During that time she lost touch with her family. Pat realized that she caused her family plenty of pain and heartache. She not only disgraced herself; she had disgraced her entire family. Pat ran away from her family and her painful past.

Five years later Pat once again became involved in an illegal act. Her past caught up with her. Pat found herself without a home or personal possessions. It was at this lowest point of her life that she realized she could not escape from her past. Pat courageously turned herself in and began serving her earlier conviction.

Something very unexpected happened while Pat was in jail. "I have found God in my life stronger than I ever imagined," she claimed. Pat realized that God had been with her to help her face the wrongs and to deal with them. While in prison Pat made new friends with people she never thought possible. "The love of God and these friends make each day bright," she said of her experience. Slowly Pat's relationship with her family was also improving, with a lot of hard work on everyone's part.

"Because of my total fall I have learned total dependence on God," Pat said, "and that has given me wings to fly once again." Pat was freed from the wrongdoing of her past and started a new life from a new perspective. We are accountable to God for the way we live our lives. Even at those times when we fail miserably, God is still there with us. God has an uncanny way of providing the right people to enter our lives at just the right moment. There are consequences to our actions, but with God's help there is also a way out.

David's problem increased because he did not include God in his problem solving. David depended on his own power to solve his problem. David thought he could take care of things himself. Uriah the Hittite arrived at the palace as he was ordered. David asked him how the battle was going, as if that was the reason he was summoned. Uriah told of the latest military news from the front. David thanked Uriah for his informative report and as a reward for his devoted service David told Uriah to go home, "Go down to your house, and wash your feet," he said. David even sent a gift home in appreciation for all his dutiful work.

There was one thing David in all his scheming did not count on and that was Uriah's loyalty. Uriah was at war and displayed a single-minded devotion to both king and nation. Uriah would not eat, he would not drink, and he would not lie at ease while the battle was raging on elsewhere. In fact, all soldiers took an oath to that effect. For those reasons, Uriah did not go home that night, but slept in the entrance of the king's house with other servants. The next morning David was told that Uriah did not go home and this infuriated the king. David asked Uriah why he didn't go home. "The ark and Israel and Judah remain in booths; and my lord Joab and the servants of my lord are camping in the open field," Uriah explained, "Shall I then go to my house to eat and to drink, and to lie with my wife? As you live, and as your soul lives, I will no do such a thing." Uriah was deadly serious with his loyalty to army and king.

It was back to the drawing board for David to once again devise a plan to solve his dilemma. David would get Uriah drunk, send him home, and let nature take its course, thus solving his problem once and for all. Before the night was over Uriah had drunk a little too much, and crashed on a couch with the servants, still not going home to be with his wife. David's plan failed once again. It seemed as though nothing would get Uriah to visit his wife, certainly not David's deceitful efforts. Uriah remained a faithful soldier.

What started out as spontaneous passion developed into a complicated plot to cover up David's sin. King David was getting desperate. Something had to be done as soon as possible. As Uriah slept David paced the floor above him devising one more sure-fire plan. Before morning David wrote a letter to General Joab. The letter contained the order to have Uriah killed, but to do it in such a way as not to raise suspicion. "Set Uriah in the forefront of the hardest fighting, and then draw back from him," David wrote, "so that he may be struck down and die." You have to feel sorry for Uriah since he carried the letter with the order for his own death. Uriah, the dutiful soldier, hand delivered his death warrant to General Joab. The order was carried out. Uriah died in battle.

David knew the ten commandments, yet still managed to break three of them. David was responsible for another man's death. As the story of David is told it would appear that he showed no sorrow, just as there was no hint of caring or love when he called Bathsheba to his palace.

This lesson teaches us that there are consequences to our actions that have a rippling effect in our lives. There are times when we think we might get away with our indiscretion, but it always seems to come out before too long. Our sinfulness cannot be ignored, but by the grace of God we can be forgiven. The good news of our faith is that we can turn our lives around and follow Jesus. It doesn't matter how badly we have messed up, or what sins we might have committed, as long as we seek forgiveness. God does not intend for anyone to suffer. Through Jesus, God calls us to begin a new life.

By anyone's definition Lupe has had a difficult, even painful life, living in the streets of Los Angeles. Lupe is only in his late thirties but looks twenty years older with considerable gray in his hair. Persons who meet him can't help but notice a tear tattooed at the corner of his left eye. Lupe admits that he has been a drug addict since he was thirteen. It wasn't all Lupe's fault either because his mother and two of his uncles were also drug addicts. His brother was serving time in prison. Lupe also has served time for his crimes. The only place Lupe felt love while growing up was with a local gang. "I knew I would die with a needle in my arm," Lupe said of his experience, feeling doomed with no way out.

It was while Lupe was living in the streets that some people from a nearby church reached out trying to help him. They shared their stories with Lupe, telling him that they too were once addicts but now had turned their lives around and were followers of Jesus. They told him if they could turn their lives around then he could, too. They would help him make that all important step. Lupe felt that God had sent these people to him. He believed that this was his last chance.

Shortly after this encounter Lupe found himself running and hiding from drug dealers. It was while he was hiding out, fearful for his very life, that he realized that he did not want to die. "God," Lupe prayed, "if you are real, give me a way out. I will serve you. I will give you my whole life." God heard his prayer and showed him the way out. Lupe embraced Jesus Christ as his Lord and Savior and turned his life around. With God's help and the help of other Christians he was able to break his deadly drug habit.[1]

---

1. Charles Colson, *The Body.* (Dallas: Word Publishing, 1992), pp. 350-351.

At The Right Place
At The Right Time

Sherry was struggling with some personal issues in her life. She would tell you that she was having a difficult time forgiving someone at work who purposely wronged her, leading to her eventual demotion. Sherry was upset with the person and could not even think of forgiving him. Her loss of income placed a financial hardship on her family. She was really struggling and trying to do what was best, but it certainly was not easy.

Sherry and her family were in church one particular Sunday morning when during time for prayer requests and concerns, one of the ushers asked if he could share his testimony. Jay shared with the congregation that he was having a hard time forgiving someone he worked with. He told of the disagreement the two of them were having and the hard feeling it had created. Jay told how he prayed about the situation, seeking the Lord's guidance in the matter. According to Jay, the Lord had convinced him that he should forgive his co-worker with whom he had a disagreement. As Jay shared his situation with the congregation it was evident that the healing process had already begun in his life. He spoke of genuine forgiveness. Jay concluded his few minutes by saying he felt the Lord wanted him to share what he had experienced.

Jay's words hit Sherry right between the eyes. Tears began forming in the corners of her eyes as she realized that this was exactly what she needed to hear that morning. It was as Jay was speaking that Sherry realized that she must forgive the person who had hurt her so badly. This was what Sherry needed to hear more than any sermon.

God has a wonderful way of working behind the scenes, bringing the right people into our lives at the time we most need to hear what they have to say. I do not believe it was a coincidence that Sherry was present that morning when Jay shared his experience.

David had also encountered the same thing, as the Lord God sent a prophet to speak the words he needed to hear after his adulterous affair with Bathsheba. To cover up his sinful action, David arranged for Bathsheba's husband, Uriah, to be murdered at the hands of the enemy. David arranged the murder so it appeared that Uriah was killed in battle, but actually the whole thing was planned out and executed by David's general, Joab. After an appropriate time of mourning her husband's death, David took Bathsheba as his wife. His plan had worked; his secret was kept. No one would suspect anything out of the ordinary. David might have thought he had gotten away with his deed, but scripture says, "The thing that David had done displeased the Lord." God knew all that David had done, including his feeble attempt to cover it up.

One morning David received a call in the honeymoon suite. Nathan was downstairs wanting to see him. It was urgent that Nathan speak with David that day. It was common practice for the king to listen to cases as a judge. No doubt Nathan had spoken with David on previous occasions about other current issues in the kingdom. When David went to see Nathan he had no idea what he wanted to talk to him about.

Nathan had a parable to tell David. I wonder if David saw Nathan's hands trembling as he began. Once there were two men, one rich and the other poor. The rich man had everything he desired including large flocks. In contrast, the poor man had little, but he was a good, hard-working man. The poor man took one little lamb and gave it to his children, who raised it as a pet. The lamb became part of that family, eating with them and even drinking out of the same cup. The poor man's children loved the little lamb as if it were a brother or sister.

One day a visitor stopped to see the rich man. Being a generous person, the rich man invited the visitor to have dinner with him that evening. But instead of taking one of his many sheep for the meal, he stole the lamb that was the children's pet from the poor man. It did not seem fair taking the poor man's lamb while the rich man had hundreds of lambs in his own pasture. The rich man took the family pet and had it served for dinner. The visitor was deceived into believing that the rich man was generous by the invitation to dinner, but actually there was a coldness in the rich man's heart who would steal and cook someone's pet. The rich man not only stole a precious possession, but he deliberately created the false impression of generosity in the process.

David, unsure why Nathan told him this story, was caught by its drama and emotion. The parable had a profound effect on David. He was outraged at the callousness of the crime; he was appalled by the whole thing. The parable did what Nathan had hoped it would. It forced David to think of others, since he was so fixated on himself. David pronounced the judgment, "As the Lord lives, the man who has done this deserves to die."

This was God's way of holding a mirror up in front of David so he could see the wrong he had committed. Sometimes we need someone to hold a mirror in front of us to see the wrongs we have committed. With great courage as well as risk Nathan told David, "You are the man." The parable Nathan told David was actually about him. He was the man who stole from the poor man in taking his wife to be his own. In effect David pronounced judgment on himself!

Jim had just started a new job in a new city in a new state. Jim and his family had just moved into a new home, welcoming the sense of a new beginning. Jim and his family had only lived in the new community a couple of months, but he had already proved to be a dedicated and hard-working member of the church. Still something was deeply bothering Jim. It was as if one day someone held a mirror up in front of him and he realized the wrong he had done. He thought a new job in a new city would erase whatever negative feelings he was carrying along with him. Jim had fallen into the trap many of us struggle with. He thought if only he had more then he would be happy, but he was not happy; he was miserable.

Jim went to speak with his pastor. Jim told his pastor that at his former job in another state he had embezzled several thousand dollars. He was able to do this without anyone even suspecting because of his position with the company. It was easy to take the money, he explained, and manipulate the books. No one at his former job ever realized any money was missing, but Jim knew and he knew God knew as well.

Jim told his pastor he wanted to make things right but was unsure what to do. He said he could no longer live with what he had done. Jim had confessed his guilt to God several times but felt God wanted him to do something about it. What Jim felt he should do was go to his former employer and confess that he had stolen money from him, though he realized that he was taking a risk. If he confessed he would be in jeopardy of losing his new job and his new home. He could even end up serving jail time that would separate him from his wife and children. When we sin, there is not always an easy way out.

Jim voluntarily turned himself in. He would spend nearly a year in jail. Jim vowed to pay back to his former employer every cent he had stolen. In spite of everything that had happened to him, this young person never felt so good. Jim sought to be right with God and made the necessary corrections. Today Jim remains optimistic about the future and is full of joy about life in general.

Mighty King David, who had an answer for everything, who thought his adulterous affair with Bathsheba was covered up and forgotten, stood in front of Nathan too dumbfounded to say anything. David might have kept his secret from others, but he could not keep it from God. God knew what David had done and was not pleased by it. There might be times when we are tempted to do something wrong, thinking we will get away with it since no one is watching, but God sees what we do. Now David was shown that God knew what he had done.

Sending Nathan to talk with David was God's way of getting David's attention. The prophet then spoke the word of God. Who was it that made David ruler over Israel in the first place? Who was it that rescued David from the hands of Saul? Who was it that gave him his master's house? Who was it who gave David victory after victory? The answer was that it was the Lord God who gave David all these things. Holding the mirror before David helped him realize that it was God who gave David everything he needed. It was God who empowered David and anointed him ruler. This was a humbling experience for David. David never could have accomplished so much if the Lord God had not been behind him.

If what God had given to David were not enough, the Lord God said, "I would have added as much more." Notice that God gave to David and that David took another man's wife. God had obviously favored David, but now in his cynical years David had forgotten God. David thought he could do it all by himself. "Why have you despised the word of the Lord, to do what is evil in his sight?" David knew the Ten Commandments, although he managed to break three of them. The truth was David reached that point in his life where he mistakenly believed he was above the law. In David's own mind he thought he could do no wrong. He was sadly mistaken because God's law applies equally to everyone; it does not matter if you are a ruler or a servant. No one is above the law of God. This was a painful lesson for David.

David relied on his own wisdom and might and forgot that it was God who empowered him in the first place. And that is what got him into trouble. He probably could not name the precise time when he stopped thinking about God.

Then came the punishment. "I will raise up trouble against you from within your own house," the Lord God informed David. David sinned and strayed from God's ways and now he would have to face the consequences. "For you did it secretly," God spoke through the prophet Nathan, "but I will do this thing before all Israel, and before the sun." When David took a long, hard look in the mirror, David realized the wrong he had done and made his confession, "I have sinned against the Lord." Even though David broke three of the Ten Commandments it was not too late for him to make a confession and repent of his wrongdoing.

In our experience, it is not always the big sins that cause our downfall. Often it is the slight unevenness of the pavement which

21

causes us to fall. Oftentimes it is the pebble in our way rather than the boulder that causes us to sin. It's the little things that lead to big things. Just ask King David. The good news of the Christian faith is that once we acknowledge our sins and seek God's forgiveness we are forgiven by Jesus and our slate is wiped clean.

The most difficult thing is to recognize our sin before we reach the point where we can not stop the consequences. In the early years of this century there was a man named Eddie. Eddie was an attorney in Chicago. He gained the nickname "Artful Eddie" for his style and slickness. Artful Eddie was one of the roars of the Roaring Twenties. He worked for the mobster Al Capone, running a dog track. It was Artful Eddie who mastered the simple technique of fixing the race by overfeeding seven dogs and betting on the eighth. Eddie had it all: wealth, status, and style. Then one day his young son held up a mirror to him and Artful Eddie did not like what he saw. Eddie decided that he wanted out of the mob, but knew it would not be easy. He turned himself in and informed on his boss Al Capone. His friends and business associates could not understand why he would do such a thing. Eddie, more than anyone, understood the consequences of turning against the mob. What could he possibly gain by turning in his boss when he already had everything he wanted and more?

There was one thing Eddie still wanted, but he knew that it would be difficult to obtain. Eddie had a son who was also named Eddie. He wanted more out of life for his son than what he represented. He wanted to clear his name so his son would have a chance to live a decent life free from the influence of mobsters. To give his son a name he would first have to clear his own and that meant considerable risk. Artful Eddie would never see his dream come true. Soon after he informed on the mob, they killed him. Two shotgun blasts would forever silence him. His friends might have wondered if it was worth it.

Young Eddie lived up to his father's sacrifice, making a name for himself. He was commissioned to Annapolis. Eddie was a pilot during the Second World War and is credited for shooting down five bombers in the Pacific and saving the life of hundreds of his crew mates. Eddie became the Navy's first flying ace. He was quite a hero. A year and a half later in 1943, Eddie was shot down and killed off the Gilbert Islands. He was posthumously awarded the Congressional Medal of Honor.

His name is one of the best known names in the world. If Artful Eddie had lived to see his son grow up he would have been proud. He had cleared his name. Today when you say the name O'Hare you do not think of gangsters, but instead you think of the international airport and of aviation heroism. He was Lieutenant Edward H. O'Hare, son of a gangster gone good.

When Life Seems
Out Of Control

During the week he was always dressed in a dark suit, a white shirt, and an expensive tie. On Saturday mornings he wore blue jeans and a flannel shirt. He was a vice president of a large corporation. He was a very successful corporate executive, but on Saturdays he was just another guy. At least that's what his neighbors thought.

As he pushed his two-year-old lawn mower out into the sun one Saturday morning, he cheerfully greeted his neighbor as she was pulling out of her driveway next door. Then he bent over to pull the starter cord. Nothing happened. He pulled it again, but nothing happened. He pulled it a third time and the mower coughed and sputtered and acted like it wanted to start, but it did not. He adjusted the choke and gave it another short, snappy pull. Again nothing happened. He pulled the starter cord another four or five times, swearing loudly with each pull of the cord. The lawn mower would not start.

Fifteen minutes later the struggle continued until, as his spouse reported, he was screaming, swearing, and carrying on like a raving maniac. Finally, he stomped into the garage, grabbed a short-handled two-pound sledgehammer, and proceeded to smash the mower into little pieces. By the time the fury subsided that corporate executive was a beaten, dejected, and broken man. The

25

driveway was strewn with jagged pieces of the lawn mower's engine and frame. Even the wheels had been beaten and smashed. The executive was found sitting on the patio, his head in his hands, sobbing uncontrollably.

Unfortunately that is an all too common experience. We are going along thinking everything is all right, without a care in the world, when suddenly, quite unexpectedly, something does not go our way and we find ourselves out of control. At those times when we are out of control we can no longer think in rational ways. So we smash a perfectly good lawn mower, we break the storm window because it doesn't go in easily, we turn over the table because we can't seem to get it level, we swear at the computer for losing a program we forgot to back-up, or we kick the dog just because we had a bad day. The list goes on and on. Something happens and we lose control, momentarily lashing out at whatever or whomever happens to be around us. On the outside everything appeared to be going all right, but deep on the inside there is an undeniable turmoil.

That's what David must have been experiencing. By outward appearances everything seemed fine, but on the inside his life was out of control. During the first years of David's reign everything had gone so well; it seemed that everything David touched turned to gold. He racked up victory after victory against a whole host of opponents. Then David let his popularity and power go to his head; he sinned and to make matters worse he tried to cover it up with murder. A prophet came early one morning to speak with David. Nathan predicted that because of his sinful act everything would soon be out of control. Sure enough, before too long David realized just how true Nathan's words would become.

David's family was in total disarray. One of David's sons brutally attacked one of his daughters. David was saddened by the incident but did nothing. Meanwhile another son, Absalom, promised revenge. Sure enough, two years later Absalom killed his half-brother who had attacked his sister. Killing his brother put Absalom next in line for his father's throne. Absalom fled his father and Jerusalem, fearful for his very life.

Three years later a wise woman paid a visit to David. This wise woman was able to see something David could not see. Oftentimes when our lives are out of control we need someone else to point out what we ourselves cannot see. We are too close to examine our lives objectively. Like Nathan, this wise woman told David a parable. Again David was in the center of the parable and again David did not realize it. She asked David to forgive his son, Absalom, and allow him to return home to Jerusalem. David agreed and Absalom returned to Jerusalem. Unfortunately, father and son were not able to completely put their differences behind them. Absalom lived in Jerusalem for two years without ever visiting his father, the king. The longer they were apart the harder it became for them ever to reconcile.

Absalom had a mean streak in him. Besides being self-centered, Absalom also had a rebellious temperament and was determined to undermine his father in every way he could. Absalom undercut his father's authority at every opportunity. Like modern day politicians, Absalom stationed himself in a heavily traveled area to speak with passersby, appealing to their nostalgia, promising simpler times which, of course, no longer existed. Absalom soon won a following and became quite popular in his own right, which did not sit well with his father. Absalom was the handsome prince whom the people adored. We find this description, "Now in all Israel there was no one to be praised so much for his beauty as Absalom; from the sole of his foot to the crown of his head there was no blemish in him."

Once in Hebron Absalom proclaimed himself king, forcing his father David along with his military advisors to flee Jerusalem for their own safety. A civil war broke out between the two sides. Everything seemed out of control. It was a deadly conflict between the fractured sides. David, who earlier was reluctant to go to battle, was eager to lead his troops, but his trusted advisor, Joab, urged him to remain safe. They could not afford to lose their king in battle, Joab explained, because then Absalom would be king. David listened to his advisors and was willing to remain behind. David stood silently by the gate as his troops marched to battle.

Before the battle, David made a personal request to Joab: "Deal gently for my sake with the young man Absalom." It was not as king that David spoke these words, but rather as a father who, despite their difference, still did not want to see any harm come to his son. Notice that David said "for my sake," not for Absalom's sake but rather for his own well being. David and his family had been through enough. The very thought of losing another child would be devastating. David spoke loudly enough for others to hear his command.

Unlike his father David, Absalom took an active part in the battle. While Absalom was riding somehow his long, beautiful hair was caught in a low branch while the mule he was riding continued on. In spite of squirming around he could not free himself. "His head caught fast in the oak, and he was left hanging between heaven and earth." Before too long some of Joab's men found Absalom. It was a strange accident, it was not as though they captured Absalom or he fell into their trap. It was just an accident that he got his head caught. It was just good fortune that they happened upon Absalom. They were unsure what to do since they had heard the king's command, so they waited for Joab. As the wise military advisor to the king, Joab would know what to do. Now was their chance to rid the kingdom forever of its rebellious, traitorous prince. The only thing was David warned Joab to "deal gently" with his son. Joab, acting out of complete loyalty for David and the kingdom, gave the order for Absalom to be killed. Joab felt he was acting in the best interest of the kingdom. He did what he had always done, acted in the way he thought would be best. Even if Absalom lost the battle but managed to escape unharmed, David's throne would never be safe. Joab knew there was no other way. There was not room for two kings in Israel. Joab watched as Absalom was killed.

The battle itself was horrible, with much bloodshed and death on both sides. Twenty thousand solders died in battle that one day. There seemed no other way to resolve this conflict; it was a battle to the finish, notwithstanding David's words to deal gently with his son. With Absalom dead, the horn blew, and the battle was over. The fighting stopped as Absalom's remaining soldiers escaped.

After experiencing pain in our lives, we are able to show a sensitivity to others going through similar pain in ways no one else can. With this heightened sensitivity we can help others avoid the pitfalls that we have experienced. I was deeply moved by Marie's story. Her only son died at seventeen of a drug overdose. Marie admits that she knew her son had a problem but really did not think he would harm himself. He is just a kid experimenting, she told herself over and over. With her son dead, this young mother was so wrapped in grief that she was unable to function for several weeks. One day, an older woman from her church came to her home and advised her to give up her constant grieving. "Give your sorrow to the Lord," she pleaded, "and he will give back one hundred-fold what you have lost." The woman prayed with Marie before leaving. She promised that she would continue praying and that she would be back to see her again.

Supported by this promise, Marie got up and began to look for ways to prevent the kind of tragedy that had happened to her son. Marie began working in a halfway house for young addicts. The young people responded to her in ways she never thought possible, due to her heightened awareness. On her bulletin board she has close to a hundred snapshots of young men and women who call her "Mom." The pain of losing her son is still there, but her life is filled with purpose as she continues helping young people.

Those who have experienced pain in their lives are able to show a greater sensitivity to others, helping them through some rough times. No one can know the pain of losing a son or daughter like someone who has experienced it. It is a parent's worst nightmare to be told a child has died. David was no different than any other parent when told such devastating news. We see the human side of David as he waited anxiously for word from the battle.

The hours seemed to drag on endlessly for him. He wanted resolution to the problem while at the same time he hoped that his son's life would be spared. As he watched, he saw a messenger approaching. "If he is alone, there are tidings in his mouth," David thought to himself as he watched the messenger approach. The first messenger was the son of one of his advisors, who told the king the news from the front. "Blessed be the Lord your God, who has delivered up the men who raised their hand against my lord the king." It was a military victory, the rebellion was once and infinitely suppressed. David would return to power. David would be the one rightful king. That was great news, but David wanted to know if his son was well. The first messenger told him he did not know; he was fearful of what the king would do if he told him his son was dead.

The second messenger arrived. "Good tidings for my lord the king!" he told David. "For the Lord has vindicated you this day, delivering you from the power of all who rose up against you." David had heard that before. "Is it well with the young man Absalom?" he asked the messenger. There must have been some reluctance as the messenger replied, "May the enemies of my lord the king, and all who rise up to do you harm, be like that young man." Those words struck David like a ton of bricks. His son Absalom was dead. It did not matter how his son had died. All that mattered was that his son was dead With the death of Absalom all of David's hopes and dreams of reconciliation vanished. There would be no reconciliation between father and son — the son was dead.

David's cry could be heard by others, "O my son Absalom, my son, my son Absalom! Would I had died instead of you, O Absalom, my son, my son!" David stood all alone in his grief. Without a doubt this was David's most authentic moment; no more plans, no more scheming, his son was dead and even though they had great differences he felt afflicted with grief.

When our lives are out of control and nothing much is making any sense, it's time to turn to God. David got himself into trouble thinking he could take care of himself. During the most crucial times in his later life, David did not turn to God for advice. David was who God wanted to lead the people. David was a complete man with a special talent for leadership. David would once again unite the people.

What is difficult for us is to know when things are getting out of hand. We think we are doing all right. Everything is going our way, then something happens that reveals there is a problem. It's at that moment that we should turn to God. Reading about the life of King David, it's easy for us to see where he went wrong. It's easy to identify his mistakes. What is hard for us to see is that what we are doing is wrong and might lead to disaster. When everything seems to be going well, it's hard to see any differently.

David Loe is a perfect example of someone who thought everything was all right. David Loe grew up in Texas and claims that he has been interested in airplanes and flying since he was in junior high school. While growing up, David had models flying from his ceiling. When persons asked him what he wanted to be when he grew up, he would always respond, a pilot. While in college David received his pilot's license. His first job was flying for a small company in Arizona. David loved what he was doing, flying a plane. His dream would be short-lived, for soon the company filed for bankruptcy and David was without a job.

David tried to get other jobs flying, but he could not find any. It was the classic example: he did not have enough experience to get the jobs he really wanted. It was impossible not to be discouraged. At a low point, David was offered a quick $5000 to fly to Mexico in a rented plane to pick up 600 pounds of marijuana. The job would be easy and it paid very well. He was lured into doing something he knew was wrong, but he was out of work and out of money. As soon as he returned from his first trip he was asked to make another trip and then another.

"That's how it all started," David explained. "I was hooked in the adventure and the cash. I began to live in the fast lane." David attended all-night parties and bought himself "expensive clothes, antique cars, a waterfront house and a sailboat." David recalls bragging to his older sister, "This is the life." He was surprised at his sister's reaction. She was not impressed. "Is that what life is about?" she asked him in disgust. "David, you need to get your life right with Jesus," she counseled. Later when David told his friends about his conversation with his sister, they all shared a good laugh together.

Then his partner was arrested and David was afraid that he too would be arrested and sent to prison. He was scared. It was at this point that his life seemed terribly out of control. He needed to speak with his family, but he was afraid that if he made any contact the phone call would be traced and the authorities would find him. He was scared and had no one to turn to. Being on the run for eight months was beginning to take its toll on David. He was a mess. One night when he was unable to sleep, he thought of all his close calls and felt that God was protecting him. The words of his sister many months before kept pounding in his head, "You've got to get right with Jesus." "How can I," David wondered, "after all the things I've done? I've run from God for so long, but now … now … is it too late? Can even a drug runner be forgiven?" he wondered that sleepless night.

The turning point came when David prayed, "God, do what you want with me. Do something! Anything!" From that moment on, David's life has changed for the better. David decided he would turn himself in to the federal marshals. He was tired of being on the run. David's punishment wasn't as bad as he thought, five years probation along with a $10,000 fine. David got right with Jesus. "When I repented, I didn't get the punishment I deserved. Instead," David claims, "I received total forgiveness."

David Loe still remembers the wrong he has done. He feels he has a responsibility to young people. It is for that reason that he speaks to churches to counsel and pray with young people who want to free their lives of the deadly influence of drugs. "I do it out of gratitude," David says.[1]

It's never too late to turn to Jesus, especially at those times when our lives seem to be totally out of control.

---

1. David Loe, "Pilot Error," *Guideposts*, September 1992, pp. 20-23.

Leaving
A Legacy

It was a once-in-a-lifetime experience for 18-year-old David Neuer when he met Pope Pius XII in the summer of 1949. David was serving in the navy and was away from home for the first time. David could see the Pope sitting on a chair carried by Swiss guards. It was one of those times when you could feel the excitement surge from the crowd. David had the opportunity to personally greet the Pope. The Pope held out his hand. "I did not know what to do," David remembers of that special day. As David shook his hand, the Pope was ushered forward. It was when the Pope was several yards ahead that David realized that there was something solid in his hand. With a loud gasp, David saw the Pope's ring in his hand. He had stolen the Pope's ring. Pope Pius XII, stopped, motioned for the Swiss guards to return. The Pope extended his hand again and David put the ring back on his finger. He smiled at the young man for a moment and then asked, "What is your name, my son?" Completely flustered David answered, "I am not Catholic, I am Methodist, and I should not be here!"

The Pope leaned forward and quietly said in perfect English, "I know you are not Catholic, and you are far from home, and you are welcome here." Again he asked the young man's name. "David Neuer, and I am from Sunbury, Pennsylvania." Then he made the sign of the cross and said, "Bless you, David Neuer from Sunbury; go in peace."

Young Solomon must have felt out of place when he became ruler. He not only felt out of place, he was overwhelmed at the large task before him. It would not be easy to fill the shoes of his father, David. It's no easy task trying to fill the shoes of a legend.

David had certainly captured the people's enthusiasm and loyalty. David won victory after victory against the enemies of the Israelites. David first gained the public spotlight when he defeated the giant, Goliath. David had reigned over Israel for forty years. David's last years were years of conflict within his family. It seemed fitting that the mighty warrior king died peacefully in his sleep in his own bed. With the news of David's death, people were heard saying, "There will never be another king like him." It would be hard for anyone to attempt to fill David's shoes.

Solomon realized how enormous the responsibility placed on his shoulders would be. Sensing the weight of the responsibility of being ruler over God's chosen people, Solomon retreated to a favorite place where he would seek out God's direction.

For those intent on finding faults with politicians, it seemed that Solomon faltered from the very beginning of his reign by going to an altar outside of Jerusalem. Solomon traveled to Gibeon, "for that was the principle high place." Gibeon was considered an important place because it once housed the famed ark of the covenant. The ancients believed that if a person wanted to communicate with God he should go to an important place, camp out overnight, and God would speak to him in a dream. This was commonly known as "incubation," intentionally sleeping in a place expecting God to communicate. It was at the very start of Solomon's reign as king that he went to Gibeon to speak with God.

The real beginning of Solomon's reign was a spiritual experience that would empower him the rest of his life. That night God appeared in a dream to Solomon. In the dream the Lord God said, "Ask what I should give you." It must have been a frightening experience. It's one thing to go somewhere expecting to talk with God; it is quite another when God actually speaks. Solomon was given a unique opportunity to make a wish. Along with this opportunity there was also responsibility. Solomon wanted to be the best king he could be, he wanted to do what God wanted him to do, and above all he wanted to obey the laws God had sent the people. Solomon had the people's best interest in mind that night when he spoke to God. That responsibility weighed heavily on Solomon's shoulders. Solomon responded by acknowledging how God had been faithful to his father David, "because he walked before you in faithfulness, in righteousness, and in uprightness of heart toward you."

Lois was going through one of those periods where she questioned her faith that we all seem to go through at one time or another. She wanted to "figure Jesus out" and began reading books on the life of Jesus as well as the Gospels. During this time of confusion, worship took on a renewed meaning in her life. During prayer time one Sunday, Lois became aware of a young couple whose fifteen-month-old daughter had a malignant brain tumor. It was Lois' turn to distribute the church flowers and she chose this young couple. Taking them the church flowers resulted in a series of visits over the next month until the young child died.

One Saturday Lois was holding Lisa in a rocking chair. She had been there about 45 minutes when she began to wonder what she was doing there. "Here was a child I had never known healthy," Lois reasoned with herself. She did not know the family that well either. "I had no obligation to be there or any reason to believe that my presence was doing anyone any good," Lois admitted. She felt very uncomfortable. Just then the little girl's body stiffened. It was almost as though she could perceive what Lois was thinking, which startled Lois. She whispered to the infant that she would stay.

"I discovered that in the process of putting aside my active search for answers and getting involved with this family," Lois said, "I no longer questioned where Jesus fit in. I discovered that I had, in fact, known Christ all along."

There are those times when the tasks loom so large before us and everything seems impossible when we need to worship God, seeking God's guidance. We do not have to travel to holy places. When life is getting the better of us, it's time for us to retreat to a quiet place to listen for the word of God in our lives. Once we remove all the distractions and interruptions from our lives we are able to communicate with God. At decisive moments in Jesus' life he would withdraw from the crowds and seek a lonely place where he would be alone so he could pray.

Solomon showed his concern for the people. Given the opportunity to make one request, Solomon asked, "Give your servant therefore an understanding mind to govern your people, able to discern between good and evil." A noble request. Solomon could have requested anything; he was granted one wish. He could have asked for selfish things and no one would have faulted him. He could have asked for a long life, or wealth, or even popularity. He could have asked God to kill all his enemies, thus preserving peace. That would certainly have made him popular. Instead of selfish desires, Solomon's greatest concern was for the people. These were no ordinary people; they were God's chosen people. It's refreshing for us to find a politician whose greatest concern was not for his own gain but for the people he represented. The king must be God's steadfast servant whose central concern must always be the people. You see, Solomon did not inherit the throne from his father David, he did not seize it for some personal gain, rather God had chosen him for the task. God had shown steadfast love to the people. Solomon wanted to be the best king he could be with concern for the people.

If God were testing the young ruler at the outset of his reign then Solomon passed the test with flying colors. Solomon requested wisdom to lead the people. Solomon's request pleased the Lord God. In the dream God responded, "Because you have asked this, and have not asked for yourself long life or riches, or for the life of your enemies, but have asked for understanding to discern what is right, I now do according to your word." God gave Solomon a discerning and wise mind. "No one like you has been given before you and no one like you shall arise after you." Solomon would be the wisest man in the world. In fact, Solomon no sooner returned to the palace when he was asked to decide a dispute between two women who both claimed the same baby as their own. Solomon in his wisdom was able to determine which woman was actually the mother and gave the child to her.

Because Solomon knew what to ask for and what to reject, God was pleased with him and granted his one request, and God exceeded it. If Solomon remained true to God's law, then God would have given others things that he never asked for. Solomon would have wealth, fame, and a long life as long as he obeyed God. "If you will walk in my ways, keeping my statutes and my commandments, as your father David walked," the Lord God told Solomon, "then I will lengthen your life." Solomon had the assurance that night that God would be with him as he set out to rule the chosen people. Solomon retreated to a quiet place seeking God's guidance. God spoke to him in a dream which would empower him the rest of his life. If Solomon remained obedient to God, then God would give him more than he ever expected.

Then Solomon awoke from his dream. It was time for him to go back to the royal palace. It was time to put into practice what God had promised him. One thing was clear to him after his divine encounter and that was that God keeps God's promises. Solomon saw in his father, King David, how God kept the covenant through some trying years, and he understood that no matter what might or might not happen, God would keep the covenant.

A Sunday school class made up of persons who had recently become Christians discussed what their newfound faith meant to them. Howard said he believed God could be trusted to give his followers "an inner peace, especially when things get really bad and you are helpless to do anything. I am not as quick to worry," Howard said. "If I have a problem I leave it in the hands of God." Cindy recalled that before she realized that God loved her when she had a problem she would always turn to people for a solution. "Now I'm not so desperate to call someone on the phone to hear them say, 'You're okay.' I still turn to people to pray for me," Cindy explained, "but God can help, too. When I get desperate, I go to church."

Another spoke of the "assurance of salvation." Faith helped another "in understanding the past part of my life and putting it in proper perspective, and in knowing that life does work out and there is eternity of peace to come."

There is not much in life that we can believe in. Everything and everyone seem to let us down, but the good news is that God will never let us down. God is faithful. Above all else, God keeps God's promises.

A Homecoming
To Remember

In the heart of our nation's capital, in sight of the Jefferson and Lincoln Memorials, is the Holocaust Memorial Museum. The Holocaust Memorial Museum is unlike any museum you are ever likely to visit, for it presents the history of the 6,000,000 Jews and millions of others who suffered and died at the hands of the Nazis during the Second World War. Upon entering the museum, visitors are issued an identity card bearing the name and picture of a Holocaust victim, matching the person's age and gender.

The exterior of the limestone and red-brick building is a sight to behold. Looking at the outside of the building, one sees symbolic references to the Holocaust, such as towers like those used to watch over prisoners in the death camps. Inside this unique museum is a staircase that looks like a railroad track that rises into a wall of black marble which leads to a door way that has been cut and set in brick in the shape of the entrance to one of the concentration camps. Among the items displayed is a rail car thought to have been used for transporting Jews to the death camps, as well as the canisters that once held the deadly insecticide used in the chambers. There are hundreds of pictures on the wall depicting what life was like for the millions of Holocaust victims. Persons can experience through photographs, films, and oral histories what those people experienced. Visiting this museum is an experience that one will not likely forget.

It is the dream of all political leaders to be remembered long after they are gone. Everyone wants to be remembered for one outstanding accomplishment. As soon as Solomon became king, he instituted an extensive building program. While his father David expanded the empire, Solomon built buildings and even whole cities where there once was only desert. He began an extensive building program unlike any the people had ever experienced. No doubt Solomon's greatest achievement was building the Temple. The Temple would be his crowning achievement. People would remember him for generations to come as the builder of the magnificent Temple.

There had been talk of building a temple to the glory of God for quite some time. The Israelites believed that the Lord God dwelled in a tent. When the Israelites were wandering through the desert and lived in tents themselves, it only made sense for the people to regard God as also dwelling in a tent. By living in a tent, God was able to travel everywhere that the people did. Wherever the people wandered God could travel with them. The people no longer lived in tents out in the desert, instead they lived in houses in villages and towns. It just did not seem right for God to dwell in a tent when the people enjoyed all the comforts of living in houses. It was only appropriate for God to have a permanent dwelling place as well. It was Solomon's goal to build a temple.

Solomon assembled the world's best architects to design a temple unlike any structure known. Work was begun with many of the Israelites laboring to complete the Temple in just seven years. The Temple was built on the threshing floor, the place where years earlier David had built an altar to worship God. The Lord God told David that although he himself would not build the Temple, one of his descendants would. Solomon chose the location which would have the greatest significance.

There was suspense as the people waited to see if God would indeed inhabit the newly built Temple. There might have been some question in the people's mind since King Solomon was the second son of David and Bathsheba. Another question in the people's mind was: Would God actually dwell in a temple designed by foreigners who worshipped pagan gods? As he dedicated the

Temple, Solomon echoed those sentiments, "But will God indeed dwell on the earth?"

The day to dedicate the newly completed Temple was truly a special day in the life of the people. Solomon delayed the dedication of the Temple for eleven months so the dedication would take place during the Festival of Booths. The Temple was dedicated during a time when the people would remember their ancestors' time in the desert. This is the most detailed dedication found in the Bible. The elders were assembled as were all the heads of the tribes as the famed ark of the covenant was brought into the Temple which would be its new, permanent home. There was much fanfare as the ark was brought forth and carefully placed in the Temple.

After the ark was in place and the priests began to leave, "a cloud filled the house of the Lord, so that the priests could not stand to minister because of the cloud; for the glory of the Lord filled the house of the Lord." The people were concerned about whether or not God would approve of the new Temple, but the answer was a resounding yes! God's very presence filled the Temple. It was an awesome experience. Some bystanders later reported that at that very moment fire shot down from heaven. Perhaps the only thing missing was a marching band and fireworks. It was certainly a sight to behold. Solomon proclaimed before God and all the people, "I have built you an exalted house, a place for you to dwell in forever."

It is comforting to know that there is a place we can go to feel God's presence. One of the places people go when they are in the midst of crises is the church. Away from their problems in the quietness of the sanctuary, they are able to search for some peace of mind. It's not unusual in city churches to find people who stop in during the day seeking some peace of mind. When life gets a little rough, when they experience a death in their family, or experience the break up of a marriage, or have difficulties with teenagers or experience health-related problems, many will go to church hoping to feel God's presence in their lives. Some just want to sit in the church while others might be crying. Still others will pray perhaps for the first time in their lives. It's comforting to know there is a place we can go to seek God's presence in our lives.

In recent years many people have returned to God, some after years of avoiding God. Don said that one of the more joyous experiences of his life came when he returned to God, after a long period of running away from him. He felt the joy of coming home to God. Don willingly admits that his running away from God was a form of adolescent rebellion. After all, Don explains, he was raised in a Christian home and attended Sunday School. It was while Don was away at college that he began to have questions. A psychology professor greatly impressed Don with his knowledge and self-confidence about human behavior. The professor was also a religious skeptic who made frequent scathing comments about the Christian faith in his lectures.

Don continued to struggle with the growing conflict in him between his faith and his admiration of the professor. It was during this time of inner struggle that Don stopped attending church. He looked to his studies to give him an understanding and meaning to life.

In his last semester of college, something happened to Don that made him want to come back to faith. Don discovered that while psychology added a good deal of informative knowledge to his life, it could not satisfy his thirst for meaning in his life. Also during that last semester he took a class from a professor who was a committed Christian. This professor showed Don that he did not have to choose between psychology and the Christian faith. Don says that he now is able to think clearly and pursue meaningful goals in rebuilding his walk with God.

The God who loves each one of us can be found in church but, of course, is not limited to one fixed place. Solomon realized this as well as he continued his prayer, "Even heaven and the highest heaven cannot contain you much less this house that I have built!" The God Solomon worshipped could not be limited or contained to one particular place. God cannot be limited or inhibited by human hands or buildings. God is beyond our control.

Solomon stood before all the people and with outstretched arms he offered a prayer to God. "O Lord, God of Israel, there is no God like you in heaven above or on earth beneath ...." This was a moment of authentic worship. With the completion of the Temple all the people would know that God is God. Solomon prayed that God would hear the prayers as well as the cries of the people especially in time of distress.

This was truly Solomon's finest moment as he dedicated the new Temple to the glory of God. At that inspired moment it was as if Solomon could see into the future when he prayed, "When a foreigner, who is not of your people Israel, comes from a distant land because of your name — for they shall hear of your great name, your mighty hand, and your outstretched arm." The Temple was so beautiful that when persons living in distant lands would see it they would be inspired. Even foreigners could learn of God's omnipotent power. The day would come when people from all over the earth would claim God as the one true God. People who would visit Jerusalem from distant cities and view this magnificent Temple would know that the God of the Israelites was the one true God. The Temple would become a link between the people and God.

The truth is that God wants to communicate with us. While no two people have the exact same experience, God does reach out to everyone. People feel the presence of God in their lives in different ways. Some even tell of feeling led into one particular church.

Diane found herself in worship for the first time in many years. For several months Diane had felt the presence of God in her life. She felt the urging, but like many people she tried to dismiss the notion. After avoiding the issue for as long as she could, Diane went to church. As the worship service began Diane once again sensed the presence of God. When the music began she says she felt lost. The opening hymn was "Praise To The Lord, The Almighty," and she managed to sing a word or two and then stopped singing altogether. "I was being battered by tidal waves of emotion," Diane claims, so she was unable to sing. Her experience of God in worship was unlike any experience she had ever had.

By the time the scripture lessons were read, Diane was hiding behind sunglasses. She was hoping no one sitting near her would notice her tears. Diane remembered the pastor as being a tall man wearing a white alb. He stood on the lowest step of the chancel, lifted his hands in greeting and began his sermon with these words,

"Why are you sitting here? Why are we all here?" To be honest, that was the question Diane was considering at that very moment. That was all it took for Diane. It was at that moment that she realized that she too was broken, burned, and bruised, and that she could not save herself. As the pastor continued with his sermon, Diane felt God's presence in a way she had never experienced or even thought possible. It was as though the pastor knew what was on her mind and spoke directly to her that morning.

Diane tried desperately to regain her composure as the service continued. At the end of the service she put her head in her arms and began crying. "Lord," she prayed," I am not worthy that you should come under my roof; but speak the word only." God spoke to Diane a word of welcome home.

Centuries before, Solomon realized that people would seek God's presence. Solomon certainly understood this as he dedicated the new Temple to the glory of God. "O Lord, God of Israel, there is no God like you in heaven above or on earth beneath, keeping covenant and steadfast love for your servants who walk before you with all their heart." That was a day the people would not soon forget. This was certainly a homecoming to remember.

Silly
Love Songs

"I can see no trace of the passions which make for deeper joy," wrote the French writer Stendhal about Americans in his 1822 essay titled "Love." "It is as if the sources of sensibility have dried up among these people," he observed. "They are just, they are rational, and they are not happy at all," he wrote. One cannot help but wonder what Stendhal would say today. It's no secret that relationships suffer in the fast-paced, impersonal world in which we live. We might rightly ask, where has all the love gone? One commentator describes the modern situation as a "bureaucratic vision" of love. Instead of risking opening one's heart to another in hopes of a joy-filled relationship, the person becomes a skilled negotiator demanding and accepting conditions for his or her personal pleasure.

We see evidence of this problem in the personal ads in local newspapers throughout the country. In recent years people have turned to the personal ads hoping to find that special person. Exhausting conventional ways of meeting people, they place ads in the newspaper and wait and hope someone will respond. One does not have to look too closely to discover the hurt and the starved affections in the persons who place the ads. One ad found a chicken delivery driver who, while making a delivery downtown, saw a woman in a denim skirt with light brown hair. No words were spoken but the man wanted to know if that woman was interested in meeting him. Another ad told of eyes meeting while one was going down the escalator and the other was going up at a crowded mall. Another described eating at a restaurant with parents and spotting someone at another table. The ad asked if the person might be interested. Still another recalled accusing another of taking all the salad from the salad bar but obviously had second thoughts, for the ad stated she would like to meet this mystery man. There are hundreds of such ads placed each week in thousands of newspapers in cities all over America. Where has all the love gone? This is a question worth considering.

Reading several personal ads prompted one woman to write to Ann Landers. Have you ever read those personal ads for people looking for dates or mates? No wonder they have to advertise in the newspaper. They all describe themselves as "attractive, physically fit, highly intelligent and fun to be with." I swear, one man actually says he's "every woman's dream." These lookers even have the gall to request specific types, such as "a Cindy Crawford look-alike." One guy doesn't want a woman with a Midwestern accent. Another guy says, "No one from New York need respond." I'm sick of reading, "I like walks on the beach, sunsets, classical music and quiet evenings at home." Nobody seems to realize that hobbies don't matter.

The writer went on to describe her marriage. In this woman's opinion what mattered most in their relationship was that they loved each other. They had different likes and dislikes but had learned to respect those differences. In that letter to Ann Landers she stated that hers was not the perfect marriage but through the years they learned to love each other and they remained very much in love with each other.

Where has all the love gone? An often overlooked gift from God to us is the ability to be in love with another person. Almost everyone at one time or another in life has been in love. The book of Song of Solomon, which is also known as the Song of Songs, is a collection of love songs or poems that celebrate being in love. If you have never read the Song of Solomon, you might be surprised at some of the imagery and the explicitness of the language. The

Song of Solomon is a collection of love songs or poems that celebrate being in love. There are no deep theological meanings behind those words; this book contains nothing more than silly love songs written by persons deeply in love with another. Being in love is a universal experience; people living in a multitude of different countries have experienced being in love. Persons throughout time have experienced being in love. Being in love is something to celebrate, something to sing about. Some of the world's best songs are love songs.

Picture the scene described in our lesson: a young woman sitting on the porch sewing alongside her mother. Her mother is talking to her, but her mind is on other things, namely being in love. She hears a voice off in the distance, puts the sewing on her lap, and looks up, thinking she heard the voice of her beloved. She hurriedly scans the horizon searching, and suddenly she sees him. "Look," she exclaims to no one in particular, "he comes, leaping upon the mountains, bounding over the hills." There is excitement in her voice as she eagerly awaits the young man she is in love with. There is something about being young and in love.

When the young man arrives at her house, he gazes at the young woman through the lattice and calls to her. "Arise, my love, my fair one, and come away." Winter has passed and spring has come. To the young man it seems that the earth has awakened at the same time his love has blossomed. There are sights and sounds of spring all around him, trees blossoming, figs ripening, birds singing. To this young man it seems that all the world joins him in his moment of great love. He says to his beloved, "The flowers appear on the earth; the time of singing has come, and the voice of the turtledove is heard in our land." Off the young couple goes to spend the day together, walking and talking, being in love with each other.

There is something about experiencing nature that draws persons closer to God. Carl was in his mid-fifties when his world seemed to cave in on him. It was when he experienced a setback at work that he began seeing a counselor. Stress was getting the best of him. In despair, Carl decided to take some time off of work and hike along Sky Line Drive in Virginia. The time away from the stresses of his life would do him good. Carl took a lawn chair with him, and at one picture perfect spot he sat down and just looked at the beautiful scenery. He sat there for several hours, just looking out over the valleys.

When he continued on his way, he found a small stream. At one time there must have been a bridge across the stream, but all that was left was the cement post. Time and weather had smoothed that cement. The top of it was rounded, looking much like a chair. Carl decided to sit there for a while. It was at that moment that he felt God was speaking to him. He described the experience as being held in the arms of God. Sitting on that old bridge was like being in a cradle, in the very arms of God. It was at that moment that he once again felt he was loved by God. It was then that he felt renewed and refreshed. When Carl returned home he was a different man; the time away as well as the rest had done him good. He was determined not to fall into the same traps he had fallen into before.

"It was a prayerful atmosphere, a real haven of rest," Carl later told a friend of his experience. "The sights and sounds were God's gifts to me. I felt peace. I felt joy. And I felt my faith growing strong as I took in the majesty all around me."

The young man was calling his beloved to go with him to the mountain tops where they could experience springtime in all its glories. There's something about love that transforms people. Romantic love between two persons, who count the number of days they have been together, is exhilarating to watch. A sure sign of being in love is day-dreaming of the other person, being consumed with thoughts of the cherished one, wanting to spend each waking moment with the other, seemingly wasting time strolling in the park hand in hand.

Being in love changes a person. Knowing that you are loved is a transforming experience as well. Margaret was the kind of girl whose face you could never remember. It was not that she was ugly; if you looked hard enough behind her plain clothes and quiet manner, she was really quite good-looking. Margaret always kept to herself. She never approached anybody or offered her opinion on anything. She hardly ever laughed. Even her friends were at a loss what to do with her. No one quite knew what to say to her.

Some boys in her class decided to see what would happen if they began to treat her as if they were interested in her. They started making it a point to talk to her every chance they got. Between classes one of the boys would ask her about an assignment, at lunch some of the other boys would purposely sit with her. This was not as easy as it sounds, since Margaret was not accustomed to anyone talking with her on a regular basis. At first she did not quite know what to say. The boys kept at it, and after three or four weeks Margaret started to loosen up. One afternoon she even asked one of the boys about an idea for a term paper.

The next step in this experiment was for the boys to start dating Margaret. Bill started out by inviting her to lunch after class one day, and Mark took her to a play on campus a week or so later. After the boys' experiment had gone on for a couple of months, an amazing thing began to happen. Margaret began to look better. A few changes were easy to notice, like the way she changed her hair around and started wearing new clothes. She seemed to talk and smile more too.

When Larry found Margaret at the library one day he asked her out on a date to hear a bluegrass band. "Oh, that's really sweet of you Larry, but Mark and I are already busy next Saturday," she replied. Larry was really looking forward to going out with Margaret. "I bumbled around and came out with some kind of line about, 'Maybe some other time,' but to tell you the truth I was really disappointed," Larry said. To make matters worse, Larry says, "I have tried two more times to get a date with Margaret and she's been busy both times."

There is something about being in love and being loved that transforms or changes our lives. Being in love is something to celebrate, something to sing silly love songs about.

Proverbs 22:1-2, 8-9, 22-23

Proper 18
Pentecost 16
Ordinary Tme 23

Lasting Impressions

During his first visit to the United States, Albert Schweitzer found himself at Pennsylvania Station in New York City, waiting for a train that would take him, his wife, and some friends to Colorado. It was the first time he had seen an immense American railroad station, and there was much to do and look at while they waited. Then Schweitzer saw a broom and, in the middle of the big crowded place, quietly began to sweep up the rubbish on the ground. After a little while he realized that in the meantime the crowd had thrown down more trash. Without getting angry or criticizing others, Schweitzer continued sweeping until the time of his departure.

People at Pennsylvania Station that day probably did not even notice the man sweeping and picking up trash. Apparently no one recognized him as one of the most brilliant persons in the world at the time. On another occasion Schweitzer shared his personal philosophy of life, "Only a person who can find value in every sort of activity, and can devote himself to each one with full consciousness of duty, has the inward right to undertake some out-of-the-ordinary activity instead of that which falls naturally to his lot."

Albert Schweitzer is remembered as a human being of great integrity who, even though he was brilliant, showed concern for

51

others. In an age where role models are hard to find, we need positive examples of people who have lived their life with the utmost integrity.

The wise author of the Proverbs stated that, "A good name is to be chosen rather than great riches." According to Cervantes Proverbs are "short sentences founded upon long experience containing a truth." The assertion is that good conduct will strengthen the society in which we live while bad conduct erodes and weakens humanity. Good conduct is in harmony with God's purpose while bad conduct is living in discord without God.

We can picture the wise teacher, having lived a long life teaching young students some of the lessons he learned in life. The wise teacher wanted to pass on his lifetime of learning to future generations so they might avoid the traps he fell into. Instead of pursuing riches every waking moment of your life the wise teacher says that there is something more important, and that is a good name or reputation. A good name, correspondingly, "is better than silver or gold."

In his quest the wise teacher learned that the first discovery is that God created the world and everything in it. That breakthrough led the wise teacher to seek to live in harmony with God. To have a good name is to live in harmony with our neighbors. Such integrity requires going beyond what might normally be expected of us by continuing to show our concern for other people. It means never being too preoccupied to help someone in need or to pick up a broom. Instead of thinking too highly of ourselves and looking down on others, we should treat them with kindness and respect. There is a common thread between people who come from different backgrounds or life experiences. "The rich and the poor have this in common: the Lord is the maker of them all." We are all children of a loving God, so any human differences really do not matter after all. If we take the time to look closely enough we can find divine attributes in every person. We were all created out of the same material.

The wise teacher wanted his students to remember that there are always consequences to our actions. We might think that what we do when no one is watching is not of great importance. After all, we might argue that we are our own persons; we do not need anyone telling us what we should or should not do. Yet our actions do have a rippling effect: what we do influences another and another. It is for that reason that the wise teacher claimed, "Whoever sows injustice will reap calamity and the rod of anger will fall." The truth is that when we do something wrong eventually it will come out into the open, and in the process other people will suffer or be hurt as a result of our actions. We erroneously think that no one will ever know of our indiscretion, so we might be tempted to continue. Even if no other person ever finds out what we have done, God knows. "Whoever sows injustice will reap calamity." It's that simple.

In contrast to the person living out of harmony with God is the person seeking to pursue a life of integrity by being generous to others. According to the wise teacher, "Those who are generous are blessed, for they share their bread with the poor." When we show love and concern for other people, people less fortunate than ourselves, God promises that we will be blessed. It is a good feeling knowing that we have done the right thing in a given situation.

"We were talking casually," recalls Sudha Khristmukti of India, "when what was uppermost on my friend's mind suddenly slipped into the conversation." Sudha's friend shared that she and her husband were paying high interest rates on a house loan. They were financially struggling with two children in school. They did not know how they could possibly make it. Sudha asked how much money they needed. The amount was the exact amount that Sudha had managed to save in a bank account. "Not a penny less, not a penny more." Then Sudha remembered how it took three years to save the modest amount. "Could I give that money away?" Sudha wondered.

That night sleep was difficult as Sudha wrestled with what to do. "I thought of all the times God's grace and loving-kindness had touched and encouraged me," Sudha reflected. "How could I not reach out to this family now?" she wondered. The next morning the decision was made. The struggling family was astonished at the generosity shown them. Sudha emphasized that they could return the money only when and if they could afford to do so. There was no pressure on them to return the money.

"I thank God for the chance to show my gratitude for all God has provided for me," Sudha says of the experience. "Each of us has the opportunity to show our gratitude by giving our time, talents, and support to help others." What an example and witness for others! She was someone who learned that a good name and reputation was of greater worth than silver or gold.

Since both the rich and poor have something in common, "the Lord is the maker of them all," it would be possible at some later time to find their positions reversed. Rich persons could suddenly find themselves in dire straits while the person with less could suddenly inherit a windfall. When people of more means help out someone less fortunate than themselves, they hope that if they were ever in need that someone would help them.

Persons of greater means likewise should not take unfair advantage of other persons. The wise teacher professed, "Do not rob the poor because they are poor, or crush the afflicted at the gate; for the Lord pleads their cause and despoils of life those who despoil them." God is on the side of the down and out. The person seeking to live in harmony with God will not take from those who have less. Persons with more clout are able to use the legal system to their own advantage, oppressing or taking advantage of the poor for their own gain. The warning is clear since God is on the side of the encumbered.

John Croyle was an outstanding football player in college, having played for the University of Alabama. John played in three bowl games and was offered a lucrative professional football contract, but he turned it down. Instead of playing professional football and earning a large salary, he started a home for boys.

"I was in McDonalds," John explains, "when this guy pulled his boy by the ear and was hurting him." John felt he had to do something to help the young boy. So John went up to the man and said, "Mister, you want to see how that feels?" The man immediately let go of his son's ear.

Since John was nineteen-years-old he was concerned for the well-being of young children. John met a boy from the streets of New Orleans whose mother was a prostitute. The little boy was his mother's cash collector as well as time keeper. John became

54

friends with the boy and shared with him how he could become a Christian. The boy became a Christian and Jesus Christ changed his life. "That's when I knew we needed a home for boys," John proudly states. Several years later John met a young girl in trouble and felt led to open a home for girls as well.

"They are not bad kids," John explains. "It's just that they had been taught some things that weren't correct." Being in a more friendly environment where these children experience love, many for the first time in their lives, transforms them. John tells the children, "Now look, you've been told your whole life that you can't do this, and you can't do that, and you're bad. You're a no-account. You're a sorry person. That's not true. God don't make no junk and God doesn't make garbage and you are not a mistake."

"Over the years I've put together the staff and raised the money to create children's homes in Arkansas, Georgia, two in Tennessee, and one in Colorado. It started with one, but there were too many hurting kids for one home. We just had to start more." John Croyle has helped over 1,200 children since he started.[1]

Blessing does not come as a reward to the person who acts kindly toward others. Rather generosity and concern for others is its own reward as John Croyle discovered in his own life. Living a life full of integrity in harmony with God is its own reward. "A good name is to be chosen rather than great riches, and favor is better than silver or gold." Living in harmony with God, caring for others comes naturally and gives us that long sought after sense of peace of mind.

---

1. Robert Schuller, *Power Thoughts,* (New York: HarperCollinsPublishers, 1993), pp. 152-154.

55

Clear
Channel Voice

One rather frustrating Sunday morning the teacher of the junior high class decided to try a little experiment with her students. What made the morning difficult was that some of the students were having a hard time concentrating on the lesson while other students were struggling to keep quiet. The teacher asked for three volunteers, explaining that all they had to do was talk, which certainly would not seem to be a difficult task for thirteen and fourteen year olds. Of the three students who volunteered, one was a talkative girl other classmates affectionately nicknamed "Motor-mouth." Her consuming interest was hair styles along with the latest fashions. She would have no difficulty talking. The boy who volunteered was interested in sports; he would share the latest scores and the statistics of his favorite teams. He would have no difficulty talking either. The third student who volunteered was more reserved but with some persuading agreed to participate.

The three students stood before the others and were given final instructions: all they had to do was talk for two minutes without stopping. The only catch was that all three had to talk at the same time. The teacher, looking at her watch, told the students to begin talking. The first girl began predictably talking about the latest fashions, including what was "hot" and in style and what was not. The second student began a play-by-play account of the baseball game he had watched the evening before. The third student told of coming to church that morning with his family and seeing a car broken down on the side of the road.

When the two minutes were up, the out-of-breath students stopped talking. When the teacher asked the rest of the class what they heard, the students were somewhat puzzled. No one could recall in detail what the three had said at the same time. Some picked up parts of what the three said, but no one could recall what all three had said. There were some in the class who listened closely to what one student said and were able to recall with some accuracy what was said, but no one knew what all three had said.

Then came time for the lesson. The wise teacher explained to the class that in life there will always be many voices crying out for attention. The students themselves would have to choose which voices they would listen to. This was one lesson that the students would remember for a long time.

Long ago there was another teacher with students distracted by other voices. These students' classroom was the busy marketplace. The teacher gathered students around the city gate and began to teach. The marketplace was a busy place with swarms of activity going on all around them. The students could not help but be distracted; some were more interested in what was going on around them than what their wise teacher was teaching them. This ancient teacher was very wise and creative with his teaching methods. Some of the young men in that class were interested in the women calling out in the street, so this creative teacher personified or embodied wisdom as a woman calling out in the street, vying for attention.

"How long, O simple ones," the voice of wisdom calls out, "will you love being simple?" The students were more interested in what was going on around them than their teacher. The simple person referred to someone who intentionally avoided wisdom or knowledge. The simple person did not suffer from any learning disability. The wise teacher wanted his students to realize that they were paying too much attention to the wrong voices. In addition, the wise teacher wanted his students to understand that there would be consequences in later life, due to their lack of attention now. "I will pour out my thoughts to you," wisdom says. "I will make my words known to you." From a wealth of knowledge the wise teacher enlightened his student. What was being taught was important, but there were too many distractions for the students to pay close attention. If they failed to gain wisdom, the day would come when these students would fall flat on their faces. At that time the wise teacher "will laugh at your calamity; I will mock when panic strikes you." On that day it will be too late. Disaster surely will strike.

It is no secret that there are many voices in our world competing for our attention. There are many nonessential activities that lead us away from God and Jesus. When we fall into the trap of listening to these other voices we have a hard time hearing the voice of God in our lives. It's not that God whispers so softly to us that we cannot hear. It's that there are so many voices competing for our attention that God's voice is frequently drowned out. We do not always hear God in our busy lives.

"There was a time in my life when it seemed to me that things could get no worse," Carl candidly admits. Carl and his wife were separated, and to add to his problems he was out of work. "I had not been going to church," Carl says, "and I felt sure that I had slipped out of God's grace." Then one day while using a friend's telephone, he noticed a painting hanging on a nearby wall. As he looked at the painting he stopped talking mid-sentence. His eyes locked on the painting of a sheep that had strayed from the flock and fallen over the side of a ledge. The wandering animal was unable to climb back up on its own.

Carl recalls that his heart melted as he looked at the shepherd of the flock bent over the ledge, straining with arm extended to reach this lone, stray sheep. Carl quickly told the person he was speaking with on the telephone that he had to go. He hung up the phone and stood there captivated by the painting. Tears began running down Carl's face as he looked at the painting, realizing that he was the lost sheep and how very much God loved him. "This picture reminded me that each one of us and I are infinitely important to God," Carl reflects. We cannot stray so far that God will not seek us out.

Even though we may have rejected God or not heeded God's calling, it is never too late for us to return to God. Faith in God is a gift from God in the same way that wisdom is. Wisdom is a gift from God and not something we can obtain by our own efforts. The wise teacher taught, "Because they hated knowledge and did not choose the fear of the Lord ... they shall eat the fruit of their way and be sated with their own devices." Therefore when we reject the gift, we are rejecting the giver.

The beginning of wisdom is fear or reverence for the Lord God. What we learn from reading the Bible, participating in Sunday school classes, and attending worship leads to inward knowledge which is valuable. Inward knowledge in and of itself is not enough. Our inward knowledge should lead us to action. Our actions soon become habits and eventually habits produce our character.

People come to faith though many different channels. People hear the voice of God in their lives in many different ways. Not everyone hears the voice of God at a certain age; some are young while others are older. It really does not matter at what age we come to faith; what matters is that we do come to faith. The path we have traveled is not as important as our final destination. Alcoholics Anonymous has been called the underground spiritual movement of our time. The first step in recovery is acknowledging that you have a problem that you cannot solve yourself. Persons in AA are supported and encouraged by each other. It is not an uncommon experience for persons to come to faith while attending AA meetings.

Several years ago a group of Russian drug addiction experts visited the United States and attended several AA meetings. They were hoping and searching for something that could be used to fight the serious problem of alcoholism in their country. They listened to the stories people told of firsthand experiences. They talked to persons attending AA meetings. Through their research they reasoned that there was something here that could help people trapped by alcohol addictions. They could not completely figure out what the solution was.

At the end of one meeting they approached their hosts, several of whom were themselves recovering alcoholics. "We want to make alcoholics like that," the Russian experts said. "Teach us how."

The hosts smiled in gentle understanding. "Well, that's what we have been doing this evening," one responded. "You see, you learn how to be like that only by being like that."

"But," the Russians sputtered, "surely there must be something you could share with us, a technique, a certain kind of approach, some kind of trick that would make this all a little easier?"

"No," came the reply. "What you see in this room, what you want to take home with you, is spirituality, and if there is one thing that all alcoholics discover, it is that there are no shortcuts to spirituality, no techniques that can command it, and especially no 'tricks.' That's what we tried to find in the bottle, in booze, in alcohol. It did not work. What we have learned is that the only technique is what we call 'a four letter word.' It is spelled T-I-M-E."

Amid the numerous voices calling for your attention is the very voice of God. The other voices might be more flashy or glamorous or get our attention first, but the advice from Proverbs is: Do not be fooled. Eventually these other voices will lead you astray. Only by listening to the clear channel voice of God can we discover life in all its fullness. The voice of wisdom says, "Those who listen to me will be secure and will live at ease." The good news is that it is never too late for us to respond to God.

Making
A Difference

There is a movement under way today — almost underground — that is designed to help young people. It's a movement championed by mothers concerned about the challenges facing children and youth these days. Moms In Touch International began almost fifteen years ago when two Canadian mothers decided to get together with some friends to pray for their children entering junior high school. Today there are Moms in Touch groups in every state, and representatives in about 45 foreign countries.

"It's a real recognition of what is happening in society," says one of the participant mothers, Sally Simpson. Sally meets weekly in a local church with other mothers to pray for their children and their school. "Television, videos, music — all of those outside influences are affecting kids' behavior," Sally explains. "As a mom, you ask, 'What can I do to try to have an impact on what is happening in society today?' Of course, the first thing is prayer," Sally states with conviction.

"It's a group of powerful women with hearts committed to pray for their children," explained Pennsylvania Moms in Touch coordinator Kathleen Nicol. "Praying for protection for our children is vitally important," said another mother, Linda White, who serves as coordinator for eleven Moms in Touch groups in south central Pennsylvania. "God chooses the most normal, everyday person to do what God wants," Linda explained, "and that's what we are — just normal, everyday moms."

Ordinary, everyday people can and do make a difference in their community and ultimately the world. What is most important for you in your life? There are probably as many answers to that question as there are people. Consider for a moment the single most important thing in your life. If you could choose, what one thing would you want to be remembered for? There are times in our mixed-up, confused world that we lose our focus of what is of utmost importance. Our attention is drawn to less important things while what is most important is often ignored or at least neglected. Some focus exclusively on getting more money and possessions while neglecting all other aspects of their lives. Too frequently we hear of people who built business empires while at the same time their personal lives suffered, and they experienced poor health, broken marriages, and children who felt as if they did not know their parents. Or worse, the children felt unloved and unimportant. Growing up in such a situation, it's no wonder that some children find themselves in trouble.

The goal or purpose of the Book of Proverbs is to transfer wisdom to the next generation. Too little attention is given to children in our adult-oriented world. The wise teacher who is portrayed throughout the Book of Proverbs instructs young students to avoid the traps and shortcomings which he himself might have fallen into. "The fear of the Lord is the beginning of knowledge; fools despise wisdom and instruction," we find in the very first chapter of Proverbs. This principle is highlighted throughout Proverbs.

In the last chapter of Proverbs we find King Lemuel's mother instructing her son. Like all mothers, she was concerned with her son's well-being, afraid that he might lose his focus. It appeared that the young ruler was spending too much time in partying and other self-indulgent activities. His mother admonished him, "It is not for kings to drink wine, or for rulers to desire strong drink." This was one trap that his mother did not want to see her son fall into.

Following this counsel, attention was turned to finding a worthy wife for the king. As with all mothers and fathers, the monarch's mother had high hopes for her son concerning whom he would marry. She wanted the best for her son; after all he was the king. Before we dismiss these verses as either a male fantasy or a nightmare, let us listen carefully to what the ancient teachers have to say to us living in the last years of the twentieth century.

The wise person understands the influence he or she has on others. Whether we like it or not, we do influence other people, most especially persons within our family. It is our choice whether we influence them in a positive or negative way. Children see and understand more than we might admit about how their parents treat other people as well as themselves. Children perceive what is important by carefully watching their parents' actions. For mothers and fathers that often means that the way they go about mundane tasks does influence their children. The person who seeks to live the Christian life will think of his or her influence on other people and attempt to provide a positive model.

According to the last chapter of Proverbs, the worthy wife places others in her family first knowing the effect she has on others: "She does him good, and not harm, all the days of her life." The worthy spouse is able to do even the mundane tasks with joy in her heart. "She rises while it is still night and provides food for her household." This loving and caring attitude is applied to all aspects of life.

Joyce Spence is a single mother who earned a college degree, got off welfare, and has seen her seven children attend institutions of higher learning. Back in February 1975 Joyce was on maternity leave with her seventh child when she discovered that her entry level job as a telephone operator was being moved to Winston-Salem, North Carolina, some hundred miles away. Nine months pregnant, with little money, no place to live, and no promise that she would be re-hired, Joyce took a risk.

One day she rounded up her children after school and boarded a bus for a new life in a strange city. Her gamble paid off, but not without years of hard work, sacrifice, and a determination to pull herself out of poverty. "I had told my children the sacrifice of those years of hard work would be worth it." Something that most of us take for granted was a big thrill for Joyce and her children. "To be able to shop for new clothes was such a pleasure," Joyce reflects. "Prior to that, all we had were hand-me-downs."

The best was yet to come as several of her children professed faith in Jesus Christ at a summer church camp. When Joyce was hospitalized after hemorrhaging severely, her children circled her bed, knelt, and prayed for her healing. Joyce's condition seemed to improve almost immediately and she rededicated her life to Jesus Christ. Today Joyce and her family are active in a church near her home.

The worthy or capable wife "opens her mouth with wisdom, and the teaching of kindness is on her tongue." Persons striving to live the devout life realize the influence they have on others and can become a positive role model for others. Everything the wise person says will be said out of love and concern for others. We admit that acting out of love is not always easy but should ever be before us as our goal.

The worthy wife devotes her time to her husband and children and finds no time for idleness. She is well organized and always prepared for whatever might happen. "Her lamp does not go out at night," because she has made sure she has enough oil.

When we strive to live the Christian life, we will discover rewards along the way. Living the way God wants us to live is reward enough. The capable wife's rewards are also evident. "Her children rise up and call her happy; her husband too, and he praises her." What a difference that would make in the lives of our family if we would find something to praise them for at the start of every day. Most definitely we would improve the self-esteem of our children and spouse. The worthy wife sets the example and is praised. Her efforts positively affect the entire family.

Perhaps the greatest reward any parent can hope for is when a child becomes an adult and embarks on the path that leads to abundant life. All those years of showing love and concern will have paid off, when you can see it reflected in your grown children's eyes. Parents can be proud of their children.

The capable wife is no ordinary woman but rather an extraordinary one who lives by following the ideals of wisdom combined with the fear of the Lord. Proverbs gives us words to live by. "Charm is deceitful, and beauty is vain, but a woman who fears the Lord is to be praised."

Jane Fagan lives with her husband and four children in a simple ranch style house not far from where she works. While Jane is well known among her circle of friends, she is barely known by others. Jane lives a simple, unassuming life. Still, the way she has lived her life has touched others. "When our two-year-old daughter died," one of Jane's friends remarked, "Jane was the one person who got me through it. She could tell by looking at you when you needed to talk." Her friend conceded, "I could not have gotten through without her." Another friend remembers going into a dangerous premature labor with her second child, and to make matters worse her husband was out of town on business. "Jane took me to the hospital and then took my daughter to live with her until my mother arrived from out of town." Marveling on their friendship and Jane's loving, caring attitude, she said, "Even friends I knew longer or was closer to did not offer to help like that."

There is more to Jane that just being helpful to others with special needs, although that is an important part of who she is. Her friends describe an indefinable radiance. "Her eyes glow when she speaks of her faith," yet another friend stated. When it comes to her religious commitment, you can just see it in her. Even if her hair is not fixed and her makeup is not put on, you look at her eyes, and she is beautiful.

Jane leads a Bible study at her church. When visitors attend her church, Jane is often the first person to speak with new people, making them feel welcome. When sickness or death occurs, Jane is often the first person to deliver a meal to the person's home. Through her various experiences Jane's faith has grown by leaps and bounds. Jane does not seek attention for what she does. Instead she prefers to work in the background, unnoticed. Jane lives out her faith, doing what some might consider unimportant, but to the people she meets what she does means so much. To the people Jane meets and helps and encourages, she is one in a million.

The author of Proverbs knew that good works seldom go completely unnoticed, "Let her works praise her in the city gates."

Stand Tall

Several years ago a police officer received a call to respond to a drowning in a small lake. Eugene was surprised since the lake at the deepest point was only about five feet deep. He assumed that the victim was a child or maybe a teenager. When he arrived he was shocked to find that a person over six feet tall had fallen out of a boat and drowned in five feet of water. He imagined him thrashing and fighting the water until he was completely exhausted and "all hope of being saved was at last abandoned." What makes this such a tragedy is that if only the man had been able to stand up, he would not have drowned.

Often when the storms of life assail us, we look for answers all around us but ignore our own God-given resources and strengths, like the six-foot individual who drowns in five feet of water. Many times the answers and solutions we seek are within us. We compound the problem when we look for difficult or complex solutions, when what is needed is often quite simple and within our grasp.

There are times in our lives when we need to stand on our own God-given two feet. God has given us the ability and knowledge to help solve our dilemmas. God gives us the strength we need when we need it as we confront the evil forces in our world. Too many people simply dismiss any possibility of accomplishing something remarkable by saying, "Oh, I could never do that," without even trying. That is a sad commentary on too many people.

There are times in our lives when we need to stand up for what we believe. When we view something as wrong it is the responsibility of Christians to make their opinions known. The best way for great causes to fail is for good people to do nothing. "Let someone else tackle that problem. What can one person do against the system?" We hear these responses from people who then list a whole host of excuses.

Throughout the pages of the Bible we find people who were willing to stand up for what they believed. These men and women saw that something just was not right and they could no longer tolerate it. They felt they had no other choice than to take a stand. Oftentimes taking a stand places us in an unpopular light. When we take a stand we place ourselves at risk. We risk our reputation, our social standing, and occasionally even our economic well-being. Many are afraid to take a stand for precisely those reasons; they are fearful of the risks involved. It is easier to sit back and do nothing than to stick your neck out. When you stick your neck out, you risk having someone chop it off.

Word had reached Queen Esther that a plot had been devised to kill all the Jews. Esther was orphaned as a child and raised by her uncle Mordecai. Soon after Esther became queen, Mordecai overheard a conversation concerning a plot to kill the king. The king had a practice of writing down the names of persons who did him favors, which would pay off handsomely for Mordecai in the future. Now Mordecai told Esther the latest news that all the Jews were to be killed. This plot was devised by one of the king's closest advisors, Haman. Mordecai told Esther that she was the only hope for her people, the Jews. She was the only person who had the power or influence to stop this evil plan. Something had to be done, but what could any one person do? Would anyone be brave enough to confront the powerful king? Certainly anyone brave enough to confront the king would jeopardize his or her very life.

This information weighed so heavily on Queen Esther that she prayed and fasted for three days. Even though she was the queen, Esther could not just march into her husband's court and talk with him. It was customary for the queen, and everyone else for that matter, to wait until the king summoned them. However, Esther could not wait until the king called her; she had to see him as soon as possible. It was a matter of life and death. Esther was able to use her God-given abilities, her beauty, charm, and winsome personality to her advantage. Esther rose to the occasion and risked her life by confronting the king.

The person devising this horrible plan, Haman, was one of the king's most trusted advisors. It was one thing to warn the king about some fanatic plotting against him, but it was quite another to warn the king that his most trusted advisor had devised a plan to kill her people. Haman sought to have all the Jews killed on the thirteenth day of the month of Adar. Haman especially wanted to see Mordecai, his enemy, put to death.

The intrigue continued as the plot thickened. Esther devised a rather complicated plan. She hosted several banquets for the king and his advisors. Esther's goal was to expose this evil plot as well as Haman. Esther very effectively set up Haman. Haman suspected nothing, since he left the second banquet "happy and in good spirits."

At the third banquet everything came to a head. As the king was sipping wine Esther made her daring request. "What is your petition, Queen Esther?" the king asked. "It shall be granted you. Even to half of my kingdom, it shall be fulfilled," he promised blindly. This was the moment that Esther was waiting for. "If I have won your favor, O king, and if it pleases the king, let my life be given me — that is my petition — and the lives of my people — that is my request." She made her petition known to the king in the presence of Haman. The scene had all the ingredients to be explosive. Everyone was having a great time at the banquet. Esther engaged the king in what he thought was light-hearted conversation, but it quickly turned deadly serious.

Esther reminds us that there are times when we need to take risks. There are times when we have no other option than to stand up for what we believe to be true, even if that means placing ourselves at risk. When we take a stand, our actions might help other people.

After twelve years in prison for armed robbery and burglary, Joe Bates was paroled. He knew finding full-time employment would not be easy. After all, who would want to hire an ex-convict? For three months Joe searched to find employment unsuccessfully. Joe became discouraged and depressed. He was ready to give up when he heard about a Tennessee businessperson named Henry Harrison. Henry was someone who took the words of Jesus to heart. He was a dedicated Christian who had the reputation of being willing to give someone a second chance. Henry Harrison hired Joe Bates to work at his company, Concrete Products.

All Joe needed was a second chance. Joe has worked for Mr. Harrison for almost three years and has become one of his most loyal and dedicated employees. A reporter asked Mr. Harrison why a responsible businessperson like himself would hire someone like Joe. "I teach Sunday school," Henry Harrison replied, "but I began to feel that it was not adequate just to teach every Sunday morning if what I teach is not incorporated into my own life and conduct."

In the past five years Mr. Harrison has employed 25 former convicts at his business. "We have had many failures," Mr. Harrison admits resignedly, remembering the parolees who breached his trust by stealing company equipment and material. "But we've also had some exceedingly marvelous successes." Henry Harrison is a businessperson who is willing to take a risk and in doing so gives a precious second chance to people who have difficulty finding employment. "I am just a businessperson who is making the effort," he says.

When we reflect on our lives it just might be the risks we have taken or failed to take that best define who we are. Esther risked her very life in exposing Haman's evil intention. King Ahasuerus asked Esther, "Who is he, and where is he, who has presumed to do this?" Esther reached the point where there was no turning back, looking at the king she replied, "A foe and enemy, this wicked Haman!" Immediately upon hearing this the king was furious. He was angry that such a devious plot was formulated and almost carried out by one of his most trusted advisors.

Before the day was over Haman was hung on the very gallows that he had hoped to see Mordecai hang on. Esther had saved the lives of the Jewish people. She was willing to risk her own life to save the lives of others.

A festival was in order, which is still celebrated by Jews today, called Purim. The Festival of Purim is a celebration of life and rest. The word carries the meaning "lots," as in the casting of lots. Purim became the festival that addresses the issues of fate and destiny. On this joyous occasion people exchange gifts. It was recorded and would forever be celebrated "as the days on which the Jews gained relief from their enemies, and as the month that had been turned for them from sorrow into gladness and from mourning into a holiday; that they should make them days of feasting and gladness, days for sending gifts of food to one another and presents to the poor."

The book of Esther challenges us to use our God-given voices and our lives for the work of God's salvation. Only God knows what might happen to us and others as a result of our faithful witness. Only God knows our destiny.

Robert was just released from a drug rehabilitation program. He vowed to turn his life around. He began attending church and before too long had accepted Jesus Christ as his Lord and Savior. Robert requested a meeting with his pastor to gain a better understanding of the Christian faith. "Now that I know what God saved you from," the pastor had said near the end of their time together, "what did he save you for?" That was one question that Robert admits he never thought of. Jesus saved him, but for what? What was his next step in his walk with Christ?

Robert prayed for direction. Several weeks later he returned to talk with his pastor. As he sat with his pastor, the pastor spoke excitedly about a drug rehabilitation clinic in Florida funded by a church and led by a reformed dealer. The pastor's dream was to start a drug rehabilitation center at this church that would help persons living near the church. The pastor felt that Robert was the perfect choice to start such a program. He encouraged Robert to be involved. "If you want me to try it," Robert said after a long pause, "I'll try it."

Robert built the program over nine months, drawing on sources personal, clinical, and spiritual. From his experiences with group therapy, he stressed mutual support and the twelve-step framework. Robert added his own personal touch as well as a Christian perspective to the program. His church continued to support him by sending him to several conferences on counseling and alcoholism. As Robert shared his past with others in the program he had started, his future began to unfold. Robert felt something important was missing in his life but was unsure what that might be. One day when he was downtown he saw a person selling colorful African cloth. Robert bought a strip that he wore to church on Sunday. The pastor was impressed and asked him to buy one hundred pieces for all the men in the church. A conversation ensued with the street vendor which eventually led to friendship. The vendor invited Robert to travel to Africa with him. Robert remembered his grandmother talking about the family roots in Africa. He decided to go with his new friend.

In a remote African village, with dirt roads and strange foods and periodic electricity, Robert spoke out to God. "What are You showing me?" he asked. "What are You saying to me? I'm going to sit still and listen."

As Robert sat in that remote village God provided him the answer he was seeking. Robert would seek to build a bond between his church and this village. This was no easy task because it would require more persons, more time, and more resources. This would become Robert's project as well as his obsession for the better part of a year.

Only God knows what might happen to us when we are willing to stand tall, to stand up for what we believe in even though there are risks involved.

Lectionary Preaching
After Pentecost

The following index will aid the user of this book in matching the correct Sunday with the appropriate text during Pentecost. All texts in this book are from the series for Lesson One, Revised Common Lectionary. (Note that the ELCA division of Lutheranism is now following the Revised Common Lectionary.) The Lutheran and Roman Catholic designations indicate days comparable to Sundays on which Revised Common Lectionary Propers are used.

(Fixed dates do not pertain to Lutheran Lectionary)

Fixed Date Lectionaries *Revised Common (including ELCA)* *and Roman Catholic*	Lutheran Lectionary *Lutheran*
The Day of Pentecost	The Day of Pentecost
The Holy Trinity	The Holy Trinity
May 29-June 4 — Proper 4, Ordinary Time 9	Pentecost 2
June 5-11 — Proper 5, Ordinary Time 10	Pentecost 3
June 12-18 — Proper 6, Ordinary Time 11	Pentecost 4
June 19-25 — Proper 7, Ordinary Time 12	Pentecost 5
June 26-July 2 — Proper 8, Ordinary Time 13	Pentecost 6
July 3-9 — Proper 9, Ordinary Time 14	Pentecost 7
July 10-16 — Proper 10, Ordinary Time 15	Pentecost 8
July 17-23 — Proper 11, Ordinary Time 16	Pentecost 9
July 24-30 — Proper 12, Ordinary Time 17	Pentecost 10
July 31-Aug. 6 — Proper 13, Ordinary Time 18	Pentecost 11
Aug. 7-13 — Proper 14, Ordinary Time 19	Pentecost 12
Aug. 14-20 — Proper 15, Ordinary Time 20	Pentecost 13
Aug. 21-27 — Proper 16, Ordinary Time 21	Pentecost 14
Aug. 28-Sept. 3 — Proper 17, Ordinary Time 22	Pentecost 15
Sept. 4-10 — Proper 18, Ordinary Time 23	Pentecost 16
Sept. 11-17 — Proper 19, Ordinary Time 24	Pentecost 17

Sept. 18-24 — Proper 20, Ordinary Time 25	Pentecost 18
Sept. 25-Oct. 1 — Proper 21, Ordinary Time 26	Pentecost 19
Oct. 2-8 — Proper 22, Ordinary Time 27	Pentecost 20
Oct. 9-15 — Proper 23, Ordinary Time 28	Pentecost 21
Oct. 16-22 — Proper 24, Ordinary Time 29	Pentecost 22
Oct. 23-29 — Proper 25, Ordinary Time 30	Pentecost 23
Oct. 30-Nov. 5 — Proper 26, Ordinary Time 31	Pentecost 24
Nov. 6-12 — Proper 27, Ordinary Time 32	Pentecost 25
Nov. 13-19 — Proper 28, Ordinary Time 33	Pentecost 26
	Pentecost 27
Nov. 20-26 — Christ the King	Christ the King

Reformation Day (or last Sunday in October) is October 31 (Revised Common, Lutheran)

All Saints' Day (or first Sunday in November) is November 1 (Revised Common, Lutheran, Roman Catholic)

Books In This Cycle B Series

Gospel Set
God's Downward Mobility
Sermons For Advent, Christmas And Epiphany
John A. Stroman

Which Way To Jesus?
Sermons For Lent And Easter
Harry N. Huxhold

Water Won't Quench The Fire
Sermons For Pentecost (First Third)
William G. Carter

Fringe, Front And Center
Sermons For Pentecost (Middle Third)
George W. Hoyer

No Box Seats In The Kingdom
Sermons For Pentecost (Last Third)
William G. Carter

First Lesson Set
Light In The Land Of Shadows
Sermons For Advent, Christmas And Epiphany
Harold C. Warlick, Jr.

Times Of Refreshing
Sermons For Lent and Easter
E. Carver McGriff

Lyrics For The Centuries
Sermons For Pentecost (First Third)
Arthur H. Kolsti

No Particular Place To Go
Sermons For Pentecost (Middle Third)
Timothy J. Smith

When Trouble Comes!
Sermons For Pentecost (Last Third)
Zan W. Holmes, Jr.